K M A Ahamed Zubair

Arwi - Arabu-Tamil - Arabic-Tamil - Lisanul Arwi

K M A Ahamed Zubair

Arwi - Arabu-Tamil - Arabic-Tamil - Lisanul Arwi

The Resilience and Revival of a Cultural Bridge of Muslim Tamils

Noor Publishing

Imprint

Cover image: www.ingimage.com

Publisher:
Noor Publishing
is a trademark of
Dodo Books Indian Ocean Ltd. and OmniScriptum S.R.L publishing group

120 High Road, East Finchley, London, N2 9ED, United Kingdom
Str. Armeneasca 28/1, office 1, Chisinau MD-2012, Republic of Moldova, Europe
Managing Directors: Ieva Konstantinova, Victoria Ursu
info@omniscriptum.com

Printed at: see last page
ISBN: 978-620-7-47914-6

Arwi | Arabu-Tamil | Arabic-Tamil | Lisanul Arwi

The Resilience and Revival of a Cultural Bridge of Muslim Tamils

Dr.K.M.A.Ahamed Zubair
Associate Professor of Arabic, The New College, Chennai 600 014, India

اللغة العربية تحمل كلمة الله، وروح محمد ﷺ، وسر الإسلام،

This work has been dedicated to the Indian Islamic Missionaries

بسم الله الرحمن الرحيم

Preface

This book delves into the rich cultural and linguistic heritage of Arwi, a unique language that evolved at the intersection of Semitic-Arabic and Dravidian-Tamil influences among Muslim communities in South India and Sri Lanka. Through a meticulous exploration of historical accounts, scholarly insights, and personal reflections, it illuminates the rise, decline, and ongoing efforts to revive Arwi in contemporary times.

Arwi, known for its blend of Arabic script with Tamil vocabulary, once flourished as a medium of religious instruction, poetry, and community identity. Over centuries, it facilitated the transmission of Islamic knowledge and cultural practices across generations. However, with the advent of modern education systems and societal shifts, Arwi faced neglect and marginalization, threatening its survival.

This book presents a comprehensive narrative of the factors contributing to the decline of Arwi, including educational reforms, cultural assimilation, and socio-economic changes. It highlights the voices of scholars, educators, and community leaders who have tirelessly advocated for the revival of Arwi, emphasizing its crucial role in preserving religious traditions and fostering cultural continuity.

Through detailed analyses of historical documents, personal testimonies, and scholarly debates, this book underscores the urgency of preserving Arwi as a vital cultural artifact and linguistic treasure. It calls upon readers to reconsider the significance of Arwi in the context of South Asian Muslim identity and encourages renewed efforts to promote its study and use in educational settings and everyday life.

Ultimately, this book aims to contribute to ongoing discussions about language revitalization, cultural heritage preservation, and the intersection of religious identity with linguistic diversity. It invites readers to engage critically with the past, present, and future of Arwi, acknowledging its enduring relevance in contemporary multicultural societies.

K M A Ahamed Zubair

Contents

Lisanul Arwi (Arabu-Tamil or Arwi)

The language known as Lisanul Arwi or Arabu-Tamil is a lasting testament to the cultural blend between the Arabs and the Tamil-speaking Muslims of Sri Lanka (Sarandib) and India. This fusion of two distinct linguistic traditions stands as one of the most significant aspects of the Arab-Sarandib and Indo-Arab cultural heritage.

Muslims cherish Arabic for three primary reasons:

(a) It is the language of the Holy Prophet;

(b) It is the language of the Holy Qur'an; and

(c) It is the language of Paradise.

In fact, the Holy Prophet commanded this love for Arabic, as reflected in the Hadith:

احِبُّوا الْعَرَبَ لِثَلاثٍ لِأَنِّي عَرَبِيٌّ وَالْقُرْآنُ عَرَبٌ وَكَلَامُ أَهْلِ الْجَنَّةِ عَرَبِي

Meaning: Love the Arabs for three things; I am an Arab, and the Holy Qur'an is in Arabic, and the language of the inhabitants of Paradise is Arabic.

To the Arabs, the term 'language' was synonymous with Arabic, which they regarded as the only true language. Consequently, they referred to all non-Arabs as 'Ajamiyyi,' which literally means 'the dumb' or 'the barbaric.'

When the Arabs arrived in Sarandib (Sri Lanka) and Tamil Nadu, they encountered Tamil, a language with an ancient and rich literary tradition, considered by some scholars to be the oldest living language in the world.

Arabic-Tamil, also known as Lisanul Arwi or simply Arwi, is a blend of Arabic and Tamil, written in the Arabic script. This unique linguistic fusion emerged through the interaction of these two cultures and provides an interesting area of study.

Origin of Arwi

Even before the advent of Islam, there were strong commercial ties between the Arabs and the regions of Sarandib and South India. When Islam arrived in Arabia, many Arabs who were already in contact with or settled in these regions became its representatives. Over time, some of the native population also converted to Islam.

As these two communities, united by their faith but speaking different languages, interacted more closely through trade, they felt the need for a common language. This need led to the gradual blending of Arabic and Tamil, resulting in the creation of Lisanul Arwi, or Arabu-Tamil.

Views on Its Origin

It's noteworthy that no scholar has thoroughly investigated the origin of Arwi.

The question of the origin of Arwi has not been thoroughly investigated until recently. It was only in the latter part of the 20th century that scholars, primarily from or residing in Sarandib, began to focus on this aspect.

Traditions in Colombo, Kayalpattinam, and Kilakarai suggest that Arwi was in use as early as the second century of the Hijrah era (eighth century CE).

Scholars hold two different views regarding the origin of Arwi. Some, like Prof. K. Abdul Ghafur, believe that it was created by the Tamil-speaking Muslims of Sarandib and Tamil Nadu, referred to as the Arwi Muslims. Others, like Hafiz Sayyid Ahmad, argue that the Arabs founded this language.

J.E. Trent, in his article "Spain and Portugal," included in *The Legacy of Islam* (edited by Sir Thomas Arnold and Alfred Gillaume, 1958), mentions a poem with Spanish words, French verse form, and Arabic script. This suggests that the Arabs may have played a significant role in the creation of Arwi. Thus, it can be concluded that the birth of Arwi was a logical result of cultural and linguistic interactions.

The birth of Arwi is likely the result of the combined efforts of both Arabs and Arwi Muslims, with each group playing a significant role in its origin and development. This language represents a synthesis of the literary and cultural achievements of both communities.

It is important to note that, apart from Arabic, neither Persian nor any other language from the surrounding regions influenced the genesis of Arwi. This is elaborated at various points throughout this study.

Arwi might have been used as early as the second century of the Hijrah era. It remained prevalent among the Muslims of coastal Sarandib and Tamil Nadu until Portuguese invaders destroyed much of the Arwi culture. James Emerson Trent, in his work on Sarandib, notes that the language was in use among the medieval Muslims of Sarandib. He also references a 15th-century

Portuguese captain, Odarado Barbasa, who provided a detailed description of the language.

Hafiz Amir Wali of Kayalpattinam is credited with reintroducing Arwi around 1600 AD after the Portuguese devastation. His tomb is located on Weavers Street in Kayalpattinam. Another notable figure, Sam Shihabuddin, significantly contributed to the growth of Arwi through his extensive writings.

Causes for Its Birth

Although Tamil has always been the primary language of Tamil-speaking Muslims, it was observed over time that:

1. M.R.M. Abdur Raheem, the compiler of the Islamic Encyclopedia in Tamil, wrote that Arabic Bengali was a precursor to Arabic Tamil (though this view is not widely supported and lacks substantial evidence).
2. Further investigation indicates that Arabic Bengali likely did not precede Arwi.

Over time, it became evident that certain terms, trends, and concepts in Tamil, influenced by Hindu religion and philosophy, conflicted with the religious beliefs, ethical concepts, and moral values of Muslims. Additionally, the Arwi Muslims, being a small minority without historical political power, felt a strong need to maintain their distinct religious and cultural identity while preserving their linguistic heritage.

Tamil and other non-Arabic words lacked the capacity to fully convey the significance of Islamic Arabic terms, which carry deep religious and spiritual connotations. Words such as Allah, Nabi, Rasul, Sahabah, Wali, and many others, along with expressions like Assalamu 'Alaykum, Insha Allah, and Masha Allah, cannot be adequately translated into Tamil or other languages. These terms are rich with meanings that translations cannot capture. Marmaduke Pickthall, in his work *The Meaning of the Glorious Qur'an*, and A.J. Arberry, in his interpretation of the Qur'an, both assert that the

Qur'an is untranslatable, reinforcing the idea that the original Arabic text has unique depth and resonance that cannot be replicated in another language.

Thus, it is said that for Islamic terms, the original is the bride, and the translation is merely a charmless shadow.

Arwi Muslims have always believed that the sincere recitation of the original Arabic text of the Holy Qur'an is crucial for the spiritual well-being of Muslims, more so than reading its translation. (For a discussion on the necessity of reading the original Arabic text of the Holy Qur'an according to its command, see appendix 21.)

Additionally, the Arwi-speaking Muslims had other motivations guiding their linguistic choices. Firstly, they needed to provide effective religious instruction in their mother tongue. Secondly, they wanted to ensure that the original form of basic Islamic terms remained intact despite using their native language as the medium of instruction.

Thirdly, many Muslims, especially women, who spoke only Tamil but couldn't read or write it, needed a way to learn to read and write their spoken language using the Arabic script, with which they were already familiar due to their ability to read the Holy Qur'an.

This need, combined with their close contact with Arab traders and immigrants, accelerated the creation of a new language. This language retained the essence and grammatical structure of spoken Tamil while adopting the Arabic script. To achieve this, certain letters that were Arabic in form but phonetically Tamil were added to the script. Additionally, Arabic letters were modified with diacritical marks to fit Tamil phonetics. The result was Lisanul Arwi, or Arwi.

Some scholars, like Dr. Nafeesa Kaleem, argue that Arwi cannot be considered a language because it is not spoken by the entire population of a region. However, it is well-documented that Arwi was spoken and written by the entire

Muslim community in Sarandib and Tamil Nadu throughout the 18th and 19th centuries, and the pre-Independence first half of the 20th century.

Others claim that Arwi is not a distinct language because it is essentially Tamil written in Arabic script. This perspective is incorrect. While Arwi uses Arabic script, it also incorporates numerous pure Arabic words. Additionally, many terms in Arwi are unique to the Arwi Muslim dialect and are not found in standard Tamil. For example, words like "Sherangai," "Shonnan," "Pishagu," and "Naththuthal" are specific to Arwi and not commonly used in Tamil.

A comparison can be made to Urdu and Hindi, which are recognized as separate languages despite having the same linguistic base derived from Hindustani. The primary distinction between them lies in their scripts and vocabulary—Hindi is more Sanskritized, while Urdu contains more words of Arabic, Persian, and Turkish origin.

Furthermore, the United Nations has recognized Arwi as one of the approved languages of the world. The UNESCO Courier, published by the United Nations Educational, Scientific and Cultural Organization, featured an article on the life of the Holy Prophet in its August-September 1981 issue. This article, written by Muhammad Yasin of Madras and annotated by Dr. Hamidullah of Paris, spans 21 pages (pages 154 to 174). A copy of this publication is preserved at Madrasatul Mawali in Kilakarai.

Excellence of Arwi

Over time, Arwi became the mother tongue of the Muslim community in Sarandib and Tamil Nadu. It evolved not only as the medium for religious instruction but also for other aspects of life.

Lisanul Arwi, or Arwi, evolved to become the primary language for the Muslim community in Sarandib and Tamil Nadu, used not only for religious instruction but also for daily activities such as business, property dealings, correspondence, and social transactions. This new language played a crucial role in preserving the cultural identity of the Arwi-speaking Muslims amidst external influences. Astonishingly, more than eighty percent of Arwi Muslims, both men and women, achieved literacy due to Arwi, which is a remarkable accomplishment.

Arwi effectively protected the cultural identity of its speakers from the powerful political influences in Sarandib and Tamil Nadu. Without Lisānul Arwi, the Muslims in these regions might have been overwhelmed by competing cultural forces, given their minority status.

Examples and Contributions

1. Even invitation cards for ceremonies and weddings were printed in Arwi (For a detailed study, see appendixes 33(a), (b), (c), and (d)).
2. Sam Shihabuddin Wali of Kayalpattinam, brother of Shaykh Sadaqatullah, wrote over 500 poetical works in Arwi, which helped

inspire religious zeal among Muslims after the Portuguese devastation.

3. Dr. A.M.H. Makeen of the University of Malaysia emphasized Arwi's role in preserving the cultural identity of the Muslim community without sacrificing their religion (FATHUD DAYYAN, Colombo: Publications Committee, Foreword p.v).
4. M.H.M. Saheed, President of the All Ceylon Arabic-Tamil Movement, noted in a letter from Karachi that, fifty to sixty years ago, over eighty percent of Muslim men and women were literate in Arwi.

Regional Variations

While Arwi thrived in Sarandib and Tamil Nadu, the situation was different in other parts of the Indian subcontinent, particularly in the North. There, the Arabicization of local languages faced significant opposition, except in a few areas where Urdu was spoken. For instance, in Dhaka in 1951, there was resistance to adopting the

Arabic script for non-Arabic Muslim languages in non-Urdu regions.

In summary, Lisanul Arwi played a pivotal role in maintaining the cultural and religious identity of the Muslim community in Sarandib and Tamil Nadu. It not only facilitated widespread literacy but also acted as a cultural shield against external influences.

Due to the adoption of Lisānul Arwi, the Arwi Muslim community in Sarandib and Tamil Nadu, which made up only seven percent of the total population, was able to preserve their religious and cultural identity without relying on external literature or the time-consuming process of learning Arabic. This language served as a cultural shield, unlike the Muslims in Burma, China, and Thailand, who lost their religious identity due to the absence of a similar separate language.

Historical Influence and Preservation Efforts

The British colonial government, recognizing the significant impact of Arwi on the local Muslim community, conducted investigations into the language. The British sought to understand its cultural and religious importance, prompting the Prince of Arcot to commission scholars like Said Aslami and Baqir Husain Raiq to study Arwi. Under the supervision of Qadi Badruddawla, the book "Sirajut Tawarikh" was created in 1830, focusing mainly on Arwi. It was translated into Persian and presented to the British Government, highlighting the language's role and various aspects of the community's life, including horticulture, archaeology, religion, and trade.

Comparison with Other Regions

In comparison, attempts to introduce the Arabic script for Bengali in East Pakistan (now Bangladesh) during a literary conference at Dhaka University in 1951 led to violent opposition, reflecting the resistance to adopting Arabic script for local languages. This incident disproves the theory that Arabic-Bengali could have been a precursor to Arabic-Tamil, as there is no evidence of such publications or manuscripts.

Literacy and Cultural Identity

More than eighty percent of Arwi Muslims, both men and women, achieved literacy solely through Arwi. This language helped them maintain their cultural identity and resist external influences, demonstrating its vital role in the community's religious and cultural life.

Arwi: A Phonetic Marvel and Literary Medium

Over time, Arwi evolved into a language capable of sophisticated literary expression, encompassing both poetry and prose. It stands out as one of the most phonetic languages globally, allowing speakers to articulate words from any language flawlessly once they've mastered Arwi.

Influence on Western Language Script

The success of Arwi likely influenced Western powers like Britain when they introduced the Roman script in their colonial territories such as India, Malaya, and East Africa. This adaptation may have been inspired by the effectiveness demonstrated by Arwi in facilitating local language communication and literary expression.

Diverse Subjects Covered in Arwi Literature

Arwi gained significant importance in religious contexts, becoming the primary medium for Islamic literature produced by Arwi Muslim scholars across Sarandib and Tamil Nadu. The literature in Arwi spans a vast array of subjects, including:

1. **Architecture**
2. **Arithmetic**
3. **Astronomy**
4. **Creed (Aqa'id)**
5. **Biography**
6. **Commentary on Hadith**
7. **Dictionary**

8. **Elegy**
9. **Eulogy**
10. **Etymology**
11. **Islamic Jurisprudence (Fara'id)**
12. **Fiction**
13. **History**
14. **Horticulture**
15. **Prayer for Rain (Istisqa)**
16. **Logic (Mantiq)**
17. **Knowledge about Divinity (Ma'rifah)**
18. **Medicine**
19. **Moral Science**
20. **Invocation (Munajat)**
21. **Satire**
22. **Sexology**
23. **Sports**
24. **Qur'anic Exegesis (Tafsir)**
25. **Proper Qur'anic Recital (Tajwid)**
26. **Mysticism (Tasawwuf)**
27. **Voyages**
28. **Warfare (Maghazi)**
29. **Yogas**

30. General Literature

Historical Recognition and Scholarly References

European awareness of Arwi's significance is evident in references found in the Encyclopaedia Britannica under 'Malayalam Literature'. Even the Portuguese in the 15th century acknowledged and studied the impact of this language. These historical insights suggest that the British adoption of the Roman script for local languages in their colonies may have been influenced by their understanding of Arwi's effectiveness.

This comprehensive coverage in various fields underscores Arwi's unique role as a language of cultural and intellectual exchange among the Arwi Muslim community.

Contributions of Arwi Muslim Savants and Religious Revival

Arwi Muslim savants from Sarandib and Tamil Nadu made significant contributions across a wide spectrum of subjects, both in Arabic and Arwi. Their monumental works are preserved in libraries such as Madrasatul 'Arttsiyyah and Madrasatul Mawali in Kilakarai, Mahdaratul Qadiriyyah in Kayalpattinam, and Madrasatul Bari in Weligama, Sarandib.

Role in Religious Revival

In Sarandib and Tamil Nadu, the revival of Islam after the cultural devastation caused by Western invasions, especially by the Portuguese, was facilitated by the extensive literature produced in Arwi. This literature played a crucial role in reinvigorating religious and cultural practices among the local Muslim communities.

Conflicting Views on Revival of Arwi

There are differing opinions regarding the revival of Arwi after Portuguese devastation. Some suggest that the inspiration for its revival came from the existence of Arabic-Malayalam among the Mapilla Muslims of Kerala. According to Roland E. Miller, the first known Arabic

Malayalam work, "Muhyiddin Mala" by Qadi Muhammad, dates back to 1607 AD. However, scholars like Rt. Rev. Robert Caldwell argue that Malayalam itself emerged as a Dravidian script language in the 17th century, stemming from Tamil.

These insights highlight the intricate historical and linguistic developments that shaped Arwi and its regional counterparts, shedding light on their profound influence on cultural and religious practices in South India and Sri Lanka.

Similarities Between Arabic Malayalam and Arwi

There are notable similarities between Arabic Malayalam and Arwi languages, as highlighted by their literary works and cultural influences:

1. **Literary Works**: Both Muhyiddin Mala in Arabic-Malayalam and Muhyiddin Malai in Arwi, authored by Sam Shihabuddin Wali, share similarities in content and style,

indicating a cultural exchange and shared literary tradition.

2. **Non-Islamic Topics**: Interestingly, the translation of the Bible exists in both Arwi and Arabic-Malayalam, marking a rare instance of non-Islamic texts being translated into these languages.
3. **Scholarly Contributions**: Scholars like Professor Mawlana Abdul Qadir Musliyar of Cannanore, Kerala, have noted the reverence with which works of Imamul 'Artus, including his Maghani in Arabic-Malayalam, are held in Kerala. This underscores the deep cultural and educational impact of these languages in the region.
4. **Educational Legacy**: 'Abdul Qadir Wali from Kotti Kollam, Kerala, known for his proficiency in both Arwi and Arabic-Malayalam, is recorded in the Kitabul Wisāda manuscript preserved at 'Artusiyyah Madrasah in Kilakarai. This manuscript contains writings by numerous saints,

addressing various religious and worldly aspects of life.

Arwi Alphabet and Its Features

The Arwi alphabet incorporates eighteen Arabic consonants that lack direct phonological equivalents in Tamil. This unique feature highlights the linguistic fusion and adaptation necessary for Arwi to effectively convey Arabic and Tamil linguistic elements.

These insights into the linguistic, cultural, and educational exchanges between Arabic Malayalam and Arwi underscore their historical significance in shaping religious and literary traditions in Kerala and Tamil Nadu.

Unique Features of Arwi Alphabet

The Arwi alphabet, essential for writing Arabic words in the Tamil script, incorporates several unique features and adaptations:

1. **Phonological Adaptations**: Arwi includes additional letters and diacritical marks to

accommodate sounds that do not exist in the standard Arabic phonological system. This ensures accurate pronunciation and preserves the intended meaning of Arabic words, crucial for maintaining religious and cultural integrity.

2. **Incorporation of Tamil Letters**: To represent Tamil phonemes not found in Arabic, Arwi utilizes modified Arabic letters with added dots or marks. This adaptation strategy allows Arwi to encompass both Arabic and Tamil linguistic elements effectively.
3. **Simplicity in Alphabet**: Despite the linguistic adaptations, Arwi maintains simplicity by utilizing a reduced set of letters. It consists of 40 letters, including 28 standard Arabic letters and 12 additional letters (including diacritical marks), which streamline the writing system compared to the 247 letters in the Tamil alphabet in its original Dravidian script form.

4. **Additional Alphabetical Feature**: In certain regions like Tamil Nadu, Sarandib, and Kerala, the Arwi script includes an additional letter known as Lam Alif Hamzah, which is counted as the 28th letter before the final letter Ya, thereby making the total 29 letters in the Arwi Arabic alphabet.

Comparative Linguistic Insight

Interestingly, while mainstream Arabic sources typically list 28 letters in the Arabic alphabet, Arwi texts from the Indian and Sarandib regions assert the presence of 29 letters, acknowledging local adaptations and regional variations in script usage and alphabet enumeration.

These adaptations and unique features highlight the dynamic evolution and functional versatility of Arwi as a medium for religious, cultural, and educational expression among Tamil-speaking Muslims in South India and Sri Lanka.

Insights into the Arwi Alphabet and Its Variations

The Arwi alphabet, with its unique adaptations and regional variations, reflects a blend of Arabic and Tamil linguistic influences, particularly notable in the enumeration and usage of certain letters:

1. **Additional Letters and Serializations**: In Arwi texts used in regions like Tamil Nadu and Sarandib, the Arabic alphabet comprises 29 letters, differing from the standard 28 letters recognized in many Arab countries. This includes the inclusion of Lam Alif Hamzah (لا) as the 28th letter, placed before the final letter Ya (ي). This variation likely stems from historical contacts and cultural exchanges between Arwi-speaking Muslims and the Arab world, possibly influenced by practices in the Gulf states.
2. **Educational and Cultural Motivations**: The addition of Lam Alif Hamzah in Arwi scripts may have been driven by educational motives, aiming to familiarize children with different forms of the Arabic letter Lam (ل)

and Hamzah (ء), known as Alif in another form. This educational approach supports broader literacy and cultural understanding within Tamil-speaking Muslim communities.

3. **Divergence from Standard Arabic Serialization**: Interestingly, while mainstream Arabic sources serialize the alphabet with Waw (و) after Nun (ن) and Ha (ه) later, Arwi texts often place Ha after Waw, deviating from the Arab convention. The reason for this divergence isn't explicitly clear from the sources reviewed, suggesting a nuanced regional adaptation within the Arwi linguistic tradition.
4. **Continued Usage and Contemporary Context**: Contemporary publications from Arab countries and even educational materials in India occasionally align with the standard 28-letter Arabic alphabet, excluding Lam Alif Hamzah and adhering to traditional serialization practices. This reflects ongoing

shifts and influences in educational standards and linguistic conventions across regions.

The variations in the Arwi alphabet, including the addition of Lam Alif Hamzah and the differing serialization of letters, highlight the dynamic evolution and localized adaptation of Arabic script within Tamil-speaking Muslim communities. These adaptations not only preserve cultural and linguistic heritage but also underscore the nuanced educational strategies employed to facilitate broader literacy and cultural cohesion among Arwi speakers.

Use of Vowel Signs in Arabic and Arwi

The usage of vowel signs in Arabic and Arwi scripts, particularly in the Tamil region, reveals an evolution influenced by historical and cultural dynamics:

1. **Transition to Persian Terms**: In the Tamil-speaking Muslim communities, the vowel signs traditionally known by their Arabic terms like Dammu, Fat-ha, and Kasra are

now commonly referred to by their Persian equivalents: paysh (for Dammu), zabar (for Fat-ha), and zayr (for Kasra). This shift likely occurred during the Muslim Renaissance period, possibly under the influence of cultural patterns prevalent during Aurangzeb's reign.

2. **Historical Context**: It is believed that prior to the Portuguese destruction in the 16th century, Arwi Muslims used Arabic terms for these vowel signs. However, with the resurgence of Muslim influence and cultural exchanges during later periods, Persian terminology gained prominence. This change might have been facilitated by figures like Madihur Rasul, who aligned terminology with the prevailing cultural norms of the time.
3. **Influence of Gulf Merchants**: Additionally, the presence of Gulf-area merchants in regions like Kilakarai and Kayalpattinam further contributed to the adoption of Persian terms. This influence likely stemmed from

trade relations and cultural exchanges between these regions and the Persian Gulf.

The adaptation of Persian terms for Arabic vowel signs in Arwi scripts reflects a historical continuum of cultural exchange and adaptation within Tamil-speaking Muslim communities. This transition not only highlights the resilience and adaptability of language but also underscores the intricate interplay between linguistic practices and socio-cultural influences over centuries.

Adoption of Persian Terms in Arwi and the Evolution of I'rab

Shaykh Jalil Muhyiddin's report from the Arabic-Tamil Conference sheds light on several significant aspects regarding the adoption of Persian terms in Arwi and the evolution of I'rab:

1. **Introduction of Persian Terms**: According to Shaykh Jalil Muhyiddin, a team of 'Ulama from North India, facilitated by Emperor Aurangzeb, played a pivotal role in teaching the Holy Qur'an to Arwi Muslims across

Tamil Nadu after the Portuguese era. This period of Islamic revival likely influenced the adoption of Persian terms for vowel sounds in Arwi.

2. **Usage of Persian Terms in I'rab**: In the context of Tanwin (تَنْوِينُ) forms (ann, inn, unn), the Persian terms Do Zabar, Do Zayr, and Do Paysh are used in Arwi for the Arabic terms Nash, Jarr, and Raf'u respectively. Additionally, Arwi has introduced two new terms, Ko Zayr and Ko Paysh, which denote long e and o sounds. These terms are believed to have been derived from Tamil, showcasing linguistic innovation within the Arwi context.
3. **Origin of "Ko" in Ko Zayr and Ko Paysh**: The term "Ko" in Ko Zayr and Ko Paysh is considered pure Arwi, influenced by Tamil linguistic conventions where "Ku" denotes a lower degree or status. This influence likely stemmed from the need to distinguish these vowel sounds in Arwi, which evolved distinctively from their Arabic counterparts.

4. **Naming of Listānul Arwi**: The language is called Listānul Arwi and not Arabic Tamil or Arabu-Tamil, indicating its unique identity and the fusion of Arabic and Tamil linguistic elements. This nomenclature underscores the historical and cultural significance of Arwi as a distinct language of expression among Tamil-speaking Muslims.

Shaykh Jalil Muhyiddin's report highlights the dynamic evolution of Arwi language and its I'rab system influenced by Persian and Tamil linguistic traditions. The adoption of Persian terms and the introduction of new terms like Ko Zayr and Ko Paysh illustrate the adaptive nature of Arwi to meet the linguistic needs of its speakers while preserving its unique cultural and religious heritage.

Origin of the Name "Lisanul Arwi"

The term "Lisanul Arwi" meaning the Arwi language seems to have its roots in historical and linguistic contexts, as uncovered by the investigations:

1. **Etymology from Telugu Influence**: In ancient times, Tamil-speaking people in Andhra Pradesh and Tamil Nadu were referred to by Telugu-speaking people as "Aruwar." The land of Tamil Nadu was known as "Aruwar Nadu" and their language as "Aruwam." This is documented in Tamil works such as Kalingattup Parani dating back to 1125 AD. This historical reference suggests that Tamil-speaking Muslims were also called "Aruwar," which likely influenced the naming of their language as "Arwi."
2. **Telugu Influence on Naming**: During periods when Tamil Nadu was under the rule of Telugu kings like Jaya Veera Raja Garu Buvich Chakravarthi, Muslim refugees arriving from places like Egypt were welcomed and integrated into the local communities. It is speculated that out of respect for the local naming conventions and

in recognition of the hospitality shown by the Telugu rulers, Muslim savants later adopted the term "Aruwar" to refer to Tamil-speaking Muslims, thereby naming their language "Lisanul Arwi" or the language of the Aruwar Muslims.

3. **Cultural and Linguistic Identity**: The adoption of the name "Lisanul Arwi" reflects the cultural amalgamation and historical interactions between different linguistic and ethnic groups in South India. It underscores the distinct identity of Arabic-influenced Tamil spoken by Muslims in the region, emphasizing its unique linguistic and cultural heritage.

The investigations into the origins of the name "Lisanul Arwi" suggest that it was derived from Telugu terms used to describe Tamil-speaking people in ancient South India. This naming convention highlights the cultural exchanges and influences that shaped the linguistic identity of Tamil-speaking Muslims, illustrating their historical integration and contribution to the diverse cultural tapestry of the region.

Further Insights into the Name "Arwi"

Apart from the historical and Telugu-influenced explanations, there are additional plausible reasons for the naming of the Arwi language:

1. **Symbolic Meaning in Arabic**: In Arabic, the word "Arwi" connotes quenching the thirst of a group of people or abundant rainfall. This symbolic association could metaphorically link to the cultural growth and preservation of identity among Arwi-speaking Muslims in South India. The language, serving to satisfy the cultural and religious needs of its speakers, may have been poetically named "Arwi" to symbolize its nurturing effect on the community.
2. **Differentiation from Arabic**: To distinguish their language from Arabic while acknowledging its affinity in sound, Tamil-speaking Muslims might have adopted the

term "Arwi." This linguistic differentiation, possibly influenced by the interchangeable nature of the Tamil letters Pa and Wa, allowed them to assert their unique cultural and linguistic identity.

3. **Modern Usage and Recognition**: Even today, Urdu-speaking Muslims in Tamil Nadu and historical texts like "Bahār-i-Azam Jahi" continue to refer to Tamil written in the Dravidian script as Arwi. This ongoing usage highlights the enduring legacy of the term and its significance in regional Muslim cultural discourse.

Cultural and Linguistic Assimilation

Throughout history, wherever Arab Muslims settled, local languages were naturally influenced by Arabic due to religious and cultural interactions. This peaceful assimilation process, driven by religious and secular necessities, contributed to the linguistic diversity and cultural richness observed in regions such as Malaysia, Indonesia, Turkey, and beyond.

The name "Arwi" carries multiple layers of significance rooted in both historical and linguistic contexts. Whether derived from ancient Telugu terms or symbolically linked to Arabic meanings, the term encapsulates the unique cultural identity and historical assimilation processes of Tamil-speaking Muslims in South India. It remains a testament to the rich tapestry of linguistic and cultural interactions that have shaped the region over centuries.

Preservation of Scripts and Romanization Issues

The preservation of scripts, especially those historically used by Muslim communities, holds significant cultural and linguistic value. Here are some insights into the issues surrounding script preservation and the pitfalls of romanization:

1. **Script Usage in Muslim Countries**: Languages like Divehi (spoken in the

Maldives) and Persian (Farsi) historically used Arabic script. This tradition continues for Farsi, but Divehi briefly adopted Roman script under a former ruler and reverted to Arabic script under President Ma'mun 'Abdul Qaiyum. This shift underscores the cultural and religious importance of script choice among Muslim communities.

2. **Concerns with Romanization**: Many Muslim-majority countries have faced pressures to romanize their scripts, including Turkey, Malaysia, and Indonesia. The adoption of Roman script can sever communities from their cultural and historical roots. It also leads to the distortion of Arabic names and terms, impacting linguistic accuracy and cultural identity.
3. **Comparison with India**: In contrast, India has successfully resisted romanization of its scripts, such as Hindi (Devanagari). This resistance is rooted in preserving cultural heritage and maintaining linguistic integrity.

4. **Example of Arwi**: Arwi, or Arabic-Tamil, was prevalent in the Arwi region until the early 20th century. Numerous Arwi manuscripts are preserved in archives like the India Office Library in London and Tamil Nadu Archives. These manuscripts highlight the historical significance of Arwi as a blend of Arabic and Tamil cultures and languages.

Challenges and Considerations

- **Cultural Integrity**: The choice of script affects how communities perceive and preserve their cultural identity. Preserving Arabic script for languages like Farsi and Divehi helps maintain cultural continuity among Muslim populations.
- **Linguistic Accuracy**: Romanization can lead to misinterpretations and distortions of original meanings, as seen in examples like Arabic names being altered in Turkish.
- **Historical Significance**: Manuscripts and books in Arwi demonstrate the rich literary

and cultural heritage of Tamil-speaking Muslims, reflecting their contributions to both Arabic and Tamil literature.

The choice of script is pivotal in preserving the linguistic and cultural heritage of Muslim communities worldwide. Resisting romanization ensures that these communities maintain a strong connection to their historical roots and accurately preserve their languages for future generations.

Arwi Periodicals, Newspapers, and the Arwi Bible

Arwi, the blend of Arabic and Tamil languages, has a rich history reflected in its periodicals, newspapers, and even in efforts to translate religious texts. Here are some notable aspects:

1. **Periodicals and Newspapers**:
   - **'Alamat Lankapuri**: This was the first Arwi newspaper, published in 1869 from Colombo by Tuan Baba Yunus, a Malay Muslim. It signifies an early milestone in

Arwi journalism, showcasing community news and editorials.

  - **'Ajā'ibul Akhbar**: A weekly published in Arwi from Madras (Triplicane) during the 1870s, contributing to local news dissemination and cultural discussions.
  - **Kashfurran 'An Qalbil Jan**: A significant Arwi weekly published from Colombo by Sayyid Muhammad Hasan ibn Muhammad Ibrahim Şahib al Qadiri of Kayalpattinam in 1889. It had editions both in Sri Lanka and Tamil Nadu, highlighting its broad readership and influence.

2. **Arwi Bible**:
  - Christian missionaries in Tamil Nadu made efforts over nearly a century to translate the Bible into Arwi. This indicates the language's prominence and acceptance among the local Muslim population, establishing it as a respected mother tongue in the region.

3. **Cultural and Literary Influence**:

   - Arwi's presence in the India Office Library in London and other archives underscores its literary and cultural significance. Manuscripts and publications in Arwi reflect the community's contributions to Arabic-Tamil literature and intellectual discourse.

Cultural Impact and Historical Significance

- **Community Identity**: Arwi served as a crucial medium for cultural expression and community cohesion among Tamil-speaking Muslims. Its newspapers and periodicals facilitated communication and shared cultural values.
- **Literary Legacy**: The presence of Arwi in various archives and libraries globally highlights its enduring literary legacy and the efforts to preserve its historical contributions.

- **Translation Efforts**: The endeavor to translate religious texts like the Bible into Arwi illustrates the language's role in religious dialogue and its acceptance beyond linguistic boundaries.

Arwi's rich history in periodicals, newspapers, and religious translations reflects its integral role in the cultural and intellectual landscape of Tamil-speaking Muslim communities. Its legacy continues to be preserved through archival materials and ongoing scholarly interest in its linguistic and literary contributions.

Historical Significance of Arwi Literature

Madinatun-Nuhas: The First Tamil (Arwi) Novel

- **Authorship**: Imamul 'Arus authored "Madinatun-Nuhas" in 1858 AD, marking it as the first novel written in Tamil by a Tamil-speaking person. This novel is significant for its cultural and literary impact, showcasing early narrative fiction in the Arwi language.

- **Cultural Milestone**: Prior to "Madinatun-Nuhas," no other Tamil or Arwi-speaking individual, whether Muslim or non-Muslim, had penned a novel in Tamil. This work stands as a testament to the literary innovation within the Tamil-speaking Muslim community.
- **Publication**: Originally written in Arwi, the novel was later translated and printed in Tamil (using the Dravidian script) in 1978, ensuring its accessibility to a broader audience and preserving its historical importance.

Arwi Writings of Saints and Scholars

- **Manuscript Heritage**: Manuscripts at Kilakarai preserve writings by esteemed Saints who were students of Kilakarai Tayka Şahib. These include figures like Hafiz Abdul Qadir Labbai 'Alim, Kunangudi Mastan Şahib, and Ammapattinam Yusuf Labbai

'Alim, reflecting their contributions to Arwi literature and religious discourse.

- **Educational Innovations**: Naina Muhammad Hadrat of Viracholam introduced Arwi as the medium of instruction at his college near Nagapattinam around 1900 AD. This pioneering effort, though short-lived due to the institution's closure, highlights early attempts to integrate Arwi into educational settings.

Cultural and Linguistic Legacy

- **Impact of Arwi**: The existence of Arwi manuscripts, novels, and educational initiatives underscores its role in preserving Tamil-speaking Muslim identity and fostering cultural development. Its use in religious and educational contexts contributed significantly to the community's cultural heritage.
- **Historical Documentation**: Arwi's documentation in various archives and libraries globally, including references in

historical texts and journals, demonstrates its enduring legacy and scholarly interest.

"Madinatun-Nuhas" and the writings of Saints in Arwi exemplify the rich literary heritage of Tamil-speaking Muslims. These works not only contribute to Tamil literature but also underscore the community's contributions to broader literary and cultural movements in South India.

Expansion and Influence of Arwi

Jawahirul Masa'il: A Rare Jurisprudence Book

- **Authorship**: Naina Muhammad Hadrat authored "Jawahirul Masa'il," a significant work on Jurisprudence in Arwi. This book represents a rare and valuable contribution to Islamic scholarship in the Arwi language, underscoring the community's engagement with religious education and legal principles.
- **Founding of Madrasah**: The institution where Naina Muhammad Hadrat taught was originally established by Shaykh Ahmad

Wali, elder brother of Şadaqatullah Appa, around 1100 AH/1688 AD, highlighting its historical roots in Islamic education within Tamil Nadu.

Geographic Reach of Arwi

- **Extent**: Arwi was extensively used across the region of Mabar, which spans from Quilon on the West Coast to Nellore on the East Coast of the Indian Peninsula. This area encompassed widespread usage of Arwi among Muslims, both in spoken and written forms.
- **Periodicals and Publications**: From the mid-19th century to the mid-20th century, numerous Arwi newspapers and magazines circulated throughout Mabar and Sarandib (Sri Lanka), reflecting the language's vibrant role in media and communication among Tamil-speaking Muslims.
- **Regional Influence**: Despite the adoption of Urdu by Labbai Muslims in the North Arcot

District from the mid-20th century onwards, Arwi continued to flourish in areas like Vaniyambadi and Ambur. Local printing presses produced books such as "Vellatti Masala" and "Arwi Munajat," which remain popular among women in the district.

Prominent Figures and Contributions

- **Literary Figures**: Eminent poets and writers like Walai Abdul Qadir of Ambur and Palli Ibrahim (also known as Qadir of Ambur) contributed significantly to Arwi literature during the early 20th century. Palli Ibrahim's notable works include "Sakhawat Nama," printed in 1919 AD in Vaniyambadi, showcasing his literary prowess and cultural influence.

Arwi Overseas Influence

- **International Presence**: In the Indonesian Manuscript Library at Jakarta, a book on Muslim Medicine dating back to 1807 AD, edited by an Arwi Muslim, is preserved. This manuscript is multilingual, written in Javanese (Javi), Persian, and Arwi, highlighting the global reach and scholarly contributions of Arwi-speaking communities.

Arwi's expansive use in education, literature, and media across South India and its international presence in places like Indonesia underscore its historical significance and enduring cultural impact among Tamil-speaking Muslims. The language continues to be celebrated for its contributions to Islamic scholarship, literature, and community identity.

Spread and Influence of Arwi in Southeast Asia

Historical Missionary Activities

- **Influence in Sumatra and Indonesia**: The presence of a book on Muslim Medicine in the Indonesian Manuscript Library at Jakarta, dating back to 1807 AD and edited by an Arwi Muslim, reflects the historical influence of South Indian missionaries in Southeast

Asia. 'Umar Wali of Kayalpattinam and 'Abdul Qadir Wali, maternal grandfather of Imamul 'Arus, were notable missionaries who contributed to the spread of Arwi and Islamic teachings in the region. Shaykh Abdul Qadir, also known as Kattānai Shaykh, from Vedalai near Kilakarai, further bolstered this influence during his mission in Atieh, Sumatra around 900 AD.

Educational Initiatives

- **Pulau Brani (Andhubar)**: During the 19th century, Habib Muhammad Maraikkayar, known as Habib Arasar of Kilakarai, directed the teaching of Arwi and Javanese (Javi) languages to the children of Arwi Muslim crew on Pulau Brani, an island near Singapore Harbour. Habib Arasar, a merchant-saint with a substantial fleet of ships, played a pivotal role in maintaining cultural and educational ties between South India and Southeast Asia.

- **Nagadeepa (Naina Theevu)**: In the Gulf of Mannar lies Nagadeepa, also known as Naina Theevu, where Labbai Naina Maraikkayar established a mosque and an Arwi school. This island served as a cultural and educational center for Arwi-speaking Muslims, highlighting the community's efforts to preserve their language and religious identity beyond the shores of South India.

Cultural Significance and Legacy

- **Merchant Influence and Maritime Trade**: Habib Arasar's extensive maritime trade network, with branches in Sarandib, Malaya, Burma, and throughout the Far East, facilitated the exchange of goods and cultural practices, including the propagation of Arwi language and Islamic teachings. His ship, the 'Mohideen Bakhsh,' which met a shipwreck off Australia, bears historical significance with its Tamil-inscribed bronze bell preserved in New Zealand.

Arwi's journey from South India to Southeast Asia underscores its role not only in religious education and cultural identity among Tamil-speaking Muslims but also in facilitating maritime trade and cross-cultural exchanges in the Indian Ocean region. The efforts of missionaries and merchants like Habib Arasar played a crucial role in maintaining and spreading Arwi language and Islamic traditions across diverse geographical and cultural landscapes.

Arwi's Influence and Presence in Burma and Beyond

Spread in Burma and Southeast Asia

- **Printing and Literary Contributions**: In Burma, Arwi language flourished, evidenced by the printing of books such as *Haqiqatul Insan* in 1882 AD at Mahmudi Press in Rangoon. Written by Shaykh 'Abul Qasim ibnu Nat-har Şahib of Valuthoor, Tamil

Nadu, this book spans 174 pages and covers various topics including Yoga Abbiyasa, incorporating Quranic verses, Hadiths, and insights from Arwi scholars. This indicates the widespread use and scholarly engagement in Arwi among Burmese Muslims.

- **Educational Institutions and Publications**: Rangoon saw the printing of three other Arwi books on different subjects, linking institutions in Akyab and Molmein. These publications underscore the educational and intellectual vigor of Arwi-speaking communities in Burma during that period.

Scholarly Contributions and Cultural Integration

- **Mawlana 'Afi al Jabarti**: A learned scholar from Syria, Mawlana 'Afi al Jabarti, settled in Kilakarai after carrying the message of Imamul 'Arus to Sarandib. Proficient in Arwi, he authored several books on diverse subjects, including a work detailing the life of

Shaykh Sadaqatullah Appa, preserved at Madrasatul Mawali in Kilakarai. His contributions enrich the anthology *Mukhammas Dhukhrul Mu'ad* compiled by Mahmud Sulayman 'Alim of Kayalpattinam.

- **Archival Presence**: Leiden University in the Netherlands houses numerous Arwi books authored by Muslims from Tamil Nadu and Sarandib, highlighting the scholarly depth and literary legacy of Arwi literature in academic institutions abroad.

Contemporary Presence and Educational Legacy

- **Continued Influence**: Arwi-speaking Muslims have established schools in Malaysia, Singapore, Burma, and Karachi (Pakistan), sustaining educational traditions and cultural identity. These institutions serve as pillars for preserving and promoting Arwi language and Islamic teachings in Southeast Asia.

Arwi's journey from South India extended its influence across Southeast Asia, particularly in Burma, where it thrived through scholarly writings, educational initiatives, and cultural integration efforts by the Arwi-speaking Muslim community. The presence of educational institutions and publications in various Southeast Asian countries underscores Arwi's enduring legacy and its role in fostering cultural exchange and religious education beyond the Indian subcontinent.

Arwi in Sarandib (Sri Lanka)

Cultural and Linguistic Significance

- **Mother Tongue Identity**: Muslims in Sarandib (Moors) claim Arwi, also known as Arabic-Tamil, as their mother tongue. This assertion is grounded in their daily practices: reading Arwi books, conducting transactions, and conversing exclusively in Arwi. This cultural affinity reflects a deep-rooted connection to their language, without any disregard for Tamil written in the Dravidian script.

- **Social and Official Usage**: Arwi extends beyond everyday life into official functions. For instance, invitations for significant events, including ceremonies inaugurated by the Prime Minister and other dignitaries, are printed in Arwi. This practice underscores the formal recognition and pride attached to their linguistic heritage. Similarly, in areas like Karaikal in Tamil Nadu, Qadis (Muslim judges) traditionally prepare marriage documents in Arwi.

Educational Landscape

- **Educational Preference**: Historically, more than eighty percent of Muslim students in Sarandib attended Arwi schools or Pallikoodams for their education. This preference is evident from statistics indicating that in 1880, while 57,000 Sinhalese students attended missionary schools, only 1,600 Muslims enrolled. The widespread attendance at Arwi schools underscores its role as a primary medium of education and knowledge dissemination among the Muslim community in Sarandib.

- **Cultural Preservation**: The choice of Arwi education over missionary institutions reflects a desire to preserve cultural and linguistic identity within the community. Despite the absence of government-sponsored secular education at the time, Arwi schools provided comprehensive learning environments that catered to the educational needs of Muslim students.

Arwi language and cultural practices thrive among Muslims in Sarandib, with its status as a mother tongue affirmed by everyday use in reading, conversation, and official communications. The educational landscape reflects a strong preference for Arwi schools, highlighting their role in nurturing cultural heritage and providing essential education tailored to the community's linguistic and religious contexts. This steadfast commitment to Arwi underscores its enduring significance in maintaining cultural identity and community cohesion among Muslims in Sarandib.

Arwi in Sarandib (Sri Lanka): Cultural and Educational Influence

Preservation of Muslim Identity

- **Language as Identity**: Muslims in Sarandib (Moors) staunchly assert Arwi, also termed as Arabic-Tamil, as their mother tongue. This identity is deeply rooted in daily practices such as reading Arwi literature, conducting transactions, and engaging in conversations exclusively in Arwi. Despite this, there is no disregard for Tamil written in the Dravidian script.
- **Official and Social Usage**: The cultural significance of Arwi extends to official functions, where invitations, including those for ceremonies inaugurated by dignitaries

such as the Prime Minister, are printed in Arwi. This practice not only affirms the formal recognition of Arwi but also underscores the community's pride in its linguistic heritage. Similarly, in areas like Karaikal in Tamil Nadu, Qadis (Muslim judges) traditionally prepare marriage documents in Arwi.

Educational Landscape

- **Preference for Arwi Schools**: Historically, more than eighty percent of Muslim students in Sarandib attended Arwi schools or Pallikoodams for their education. This preference is evident from statistics indicating that in 1880, while 57,000 Sinhalese students attended missionary schools, only 1,600 Muslims enrolled in them. The widespread attendance at Arwi schools underscores its role as a primary medium of education and knowledge dissemination among the Muslim community in Sarandib.

- **Cultural and Religious Literature**: The dominance of Arwi among Sarandib Muslims facilitated the publication of religious texts in the language. Examples include the **Mizan Malai**, composed by Shaykh Mustafa Wali of Beruwela, Sarandib, first published in 1285 AH/1868 AD. This work remains popular among Sarandib Moors, with explanatory notes in Arwi added by the author's son, Shaykh Muhammad.

Sociopolitical Context

- **Resistance to Cultural Assimilation**: Sarandib Muslims have historically resisted efforts by local Tamils to deny their Muslim identity and assimilate them into Tamil culture. This resistance aimed to protect their distinct cultural and religious practices and preserve their community's heritage.

Contributions of Educational Institutions

- **Madrasahs and Colleges**: Institutions such as Madrasatul Artusiyyah in Kilakarai, Mahdara in Kayalpattinam, and Madrasatul Bari in Sarandib played pivotal roles in promoting Arwi during the early 20th century. These institutions, guided by scholars like Khalifa Muhammad Ibrahim Wali, actively propagated Arwi despite historical challenges.
- **Foundations and Contributions**: Foundations like Zavia in Kayalpattinam, Rahmaniyyah in Adirampattinam, and Yusufiyyah in Madras significantly contributed to the development and preservation of Arwi language and culture.

Arwi language and cultural practices remain integral to the identity and heritage of Muslims in Sarandib. Its use in education, literature, and everyday communication underscores its enduring significance in maintaining cultural identity and community cohesion. The resilience of Sarandib Muslims against cultural assimilation reflects a deep-seated commitment to preserve their linguistic and religious heritage through Arwi.

Cultural and Educational Contributions of Arwi in Sarandib (Sri Lanka)

Educational Initiatives and Institutions

- **Promotion through Education**: E.L. Ibrahim Labbai Maraikayar, a prominent merchant in Sarandib, played a pivotal role in promoting Arwi. He established the organization Ma'tunatur Rahman, which funded and maintained a network of Maktabs (Pallikoodam) across Sarandib. This initiative aimed to ensure that children received religious education through books like *Tuhfatul Atfal* and *Minhatul Atfal* for the Hanafiyyi and Shafi'iyyi schools, respectively. He also founded Tarbiyyatul Atfal to oversee their proper upbringing and education.

- **Bahjatul Ibrahimiyya**: Founded in 1310 AH/1892 AD in Fort Galle, under the principalship of Colombo 'Alim Şahib, this institution actively propagated the use of Arwi. It contributed significantly to the cultural and educational landscape of Sarandib.
- **Contribution of Khalifa Muhammad Haneefa Baas**: A disciple of Imamul 'Arts, Khalifa Muhammad Haneefa Baas authored several compositions, including notable works such as *Arwiyyah* and *Artusiyyah Malai*. His literary contributions enriched the Arwi language and its cultural significance in Sarandib.

Literary and Cultural Contributions

- **Early Prose Writers**: Scholars like Qadi Jan Şahib 'Alim and Muhammad Labbai 'Alim from Pavalanagar (present-day Palayakat) in Tamil Nadu are among the pioneers who wrote Arwi books in prose. Their contributions date back to 1281 AH/1864 AD, reflecting the early literary efforts in Arwi.

- **Poetic Expressions**: Shaykh Mustafa Wali, influenced by his studies in Kayalpattinam, composed poems in Arwi to praise his spiritual master, maste 'Umar Waliyullah. This poetic tradition not only celebrated spiritual mentors but also preserved cultural values through literature.

Sociocultural Context

- **Cultural Identity**: Sarandib Muslims, known as Moors, strongly affirm Arwi (Arabic-Tamil) as their mother tongue. This affirmation is evident in their everyday practices, including reading, writing, and speaking exclusively in Arwi. Despite this, there is a mutual respect for Tamil written in the Dravidian script, highlighting a harmonious coexistence of cultural identities.

- **Resistance and Preservation**: The community's resistance against assimilation into Tamil culture underscores their efforts to preserve their distinct Muslim identity. This resistance has historical roots and is crucial for maintaining cultural heritage amidst external pressures.

Arwi language and cultural practices continue to thrive among Muslims in Sarandib, with significant contributions in education, literature, and community development. Initiatives by influential figures like E.L. Ibrahim Labbai Maraikayar and Khalifa Muhammad Haneefa Baas have played crucial roles in fostering educational institutions and enriching Arwi literature. These efforts not only preserve cultural identity but also strengthen community cohesion and pride in Sarandib's diverse cultural landscape.

Contributions and Cultural Significance of Arwi in Sarandib

Literary Contributions

- **Translation of the Holy Qur'an**: Siddi Labbai, a notable Moor from Sarandib, is credited as the first Arwi Muslim to attempt the translation of the Holy Qur'an into Arwi. While the entire translation is said to have been completed, only five parts (juz'u) have been printed and preserved.
- **Tuhfatus Sarandib**: A significant Arwi book titled *Tuhfatus Sarandib* by Hidayatullah is mentioned in the Sarandib magazine *Kalpana* (July 18, 1975). This book, dealing with religious aspects in Arwi, is preserved at the National Archives in Madras, although specific details regarding its themes and language remain elusive.

Cultural and Educational Figures

- **Siddi Labbai**: Known for his book series *Hidayatul Qasimiyyah*, aimed at teaching Arabic, Siddi Labbai dedicated his life to serving Arwi through educational initiatives and literature. His contributions helped in promoting Arabic education among the Sarandib community.

- **Hasan ibnu 'Uthman Wali**: Regarded as the first Moorish Saint of Sarandib, Hasan ibnu 'Uthman Wali received his education in Kayalpattinam under Shaykhuna Labbai 'Alim. His influence and teachings contributed significantly to the cultural and spiritual fabric of Sarandib, despite the challenges posed by historical destruction and Portuguese suppression.

Cultural Preservation and Challenges

- **Cultural Preservation**: Sarandib, despite historical challenges such as Portuguese destruction and attempts to erase Islamic monuments, maintains its cultural heritage through revered figures like Hasan ibnu 'Uthman Wali. Shrines dedicated to various Saints serve as cultural landmarks, even though many lack dates or tombstones due to historical damage.

Arwi language and literature continue to play a crucial role in Sarandib's cultural identity and educational framework. Figures like Siddi Labbai and Hasan ibnu 'Uthman Wali exemplify the resilience and dedication of Sarandib's Muslim community in preserving their language, religious teachings, and cultural heritage. Their contributions, including literary works and educational initiatives, underscore the enduring significance of Arwi in shaping Sarandib's cultural landscape despite historical adversities.

Prominent Figures and Contributions in Arwi Literature

Shaykhna Labbai 'Alim of Kayalpattinam

- **Literary Contributions**: Shaykhna Labbai 'Alim, grandson of Sadaqatullah Appa and mentor to many, composed numerous poems in both Arwi and Arabic. His works, including the poem *Razzanatul 'Ibn*, demonstrate his skill in translating Tamil moral poems into Arwi, highlighting his literary prowess and cultural contributions.

Kashawatta Muhammad Labbai 'Alim of Sarandib

- **Poetic Works**: Known as a student of Tayka Sahib of Kayalpattinam and contemporary of Imamul 'Arts, Kashawatta Muhammad Labbai 'Alim authored several Arwi and Arabic poems, primarily praising his teacher Tayka Sahib. His poetic endeavors exemplify his dedication to preserving cultural and educational values through literature.

Habib Muhammad Labbai 'Alim of Eravur

- **Historical Influence**: Descendant of Javanese 'Ulama brought to Sarandib by the Dutch, Habib Muhammad Labbai 'Alim's family transitioned to speaking and writing in Arwi under the influence of Imamul 'Arts. This shift reflects the cultural and linguistic adaptations influenced by historical contexts and educational developments.

Oadakkarai 'Alim of Kattankudi

- **Literary Legacy**: Known for possessing the largest private collection of Arwi books, Oadakkarai 'Alim's library was a testament to his commitment to preserving Arwi literature. His extensive collection underscores the importance of personal initiatives in safeguarding cultural and educational heritage.

Habib Muhammad Alim of Mawilmada

- **Educational Contributions**: A student of Kona Shaykh 'Abdul Qadir 'Alim at Adirampattinam, Habib Muhammad Alim initiated his career as an Arwi writer and continued his literary pursuits as the principal of Bahjatul Ibrahimiyya in Fort Galle. His advocacy for Arwi literature in challenging circumstances highlights his dedication to educational advancement and cultural preservation.

These individuals, through their literary works and educational contributions, significantly shaped the cultural and educational landscape of their respective communities. Their efforts in promoting Arwi language and literature not only preserved cultural identity but also fostered educational development among future generations. Their legacies continue to inspire and educate, emphasizing the enduring importance of Arwi in both historical and contemporary contexts.

Arwi and Its Cultural Significance

European Conversion and Proficiency in Arwi

- **Historical Anecdote**: Imamul 'Artus documented the conversion of Assistant Government Agent La Messure to Islam at the hands of Muhammad Hanifah in Maradana. La Messure, proficient in Arwi despite being unable to read or write Tamil in the Dravidian script, settled in Sarandib's eastern province after resigning from government service. His story highlights the cultural integration and linguistic prowess associated with Arwi among diverse communities.

All Ceylon Arabic-Tamil Movement

- **Cultural Advocacy**: Founded by M.H.M. Saheed in 1963, the All Ceylon Arabic-Tamil Movement aimed to establish recognition for Arwi as the mother-tongue of Moors in Sarandib. Despite the efforts, a resolution led by Sir Razik Fareed at the All Ceylon Muslim Educational Conference in 1963 to officially recognize Arwi faced challenges. Concerns over its impact on secular education and inadequate resources for producing Arwi-based secular books hindered its adoption.

Arwi and Swahili Connections

- **Cultural Parallels**: A.M.A. 'Aziz noted similarities between the Swahili book *Utendi Wa Mwana Kupona* and the Arwi work *Penn Buthi Malai* by Sam. This discovery underscores the cultural exchanges and influences between Arwi-speaking communities and Swahili-speaking regions of East Africa. Both texts offer advice to women, reflecting shared cultural values despite geographic and linguistic differences.

Arwi's historical significance transcends linguistic boundaries, influencing cultural identities and educational movements. From European conversions in Sarandib to advocacy for recognition as a mother-tongue and cultural parallels with Swahili literature, Arwi continues to play a vital role in preserving cultural heritage and fostering intercultural exchanges. These narratives highlight its enduring relevance and the richness of Arwi literature in global contexts.

Shihabuddin Wali and *Rasul Malai*

Shihabuddin Wali, renowned for his work *Rasul Malai*, holds a significant place among the Moors in Sarandib, particularly cherished by women and recognized as one of the earliest available Arwi books.

Comparative Study of Swahili and Arwi

A comparative analysis conducted by 'Aziz revealed intriguing similarities between Swahili and Arwi:

- **Diacritical Marks**: Both languages employ diacritical signs to modify Arabic letters, a feature facilitating linguistic flexibility and adaptation.
- **Arabic Influence**: Both Arwi and Swahili integrate Arabic vocabulary extensively, enriching their lexicons with Arabic terms.
- **Script and Grammar**: Despite using Arabic script, Arwi adheres strictly to Tamil grammar and writing conventions. Similarly, Swahili in Arabic script maintains fidelity to Bantu language grammar and style prevalent on the East African Coast.

Cultural Insights from East Africa

During a visit to East African cities such as Zanzibar, Dar-es-Salam, Arusha, and Mombasa in 1990, the writer encountered challenges in locating books in Arabic-Swahili script. British influence had seemingly suppressed and diminished the use of Arabic script in Swahili literature, with only a few awrad books accessible in Arabic. The scarcity of Arabic-Swahili script publications underscored a cultural loss resulting from colonial-era interventions.

The legacy of Shihabuddin Wali's *Rasul Malai* and the parallels drawn between Arwi and Swahili highlight their shared linguistic and cultural heritage. Despite challenges in accessing Swahili texts in Arabic script, historical guides and selective publications continue to attest to the existence and significance of Swahili literature in Arabic script. These insights illuminate the enduring influence of Arabic-script languages across diverse regions and underscore efforts to preserve and understand their cultural contributions.

Arwi and Literacy Promotion

Arwi, historically promoted through religious education institutions like Maktabs in Sarandib and Tamil Nadu, played a crucial role in ensuring primary literacy among Muslim communities. These Maktabs operated independently, adjacent to mosques, and were sustained by Labbai teachers. They imparted foundational knowledge including the Holy Qur'an recitation (Tajwid), Islamic principles, and the life of the Prophet Muhammad.

Parents considered it a sacred duty to enroll their children in these Maktabs, thereby securing basic literacy within the Muslim population. However, with the advent of compulsory secular education and shifting parental priorities, the number of these institutions declined significantly, particularly in urban areas. Modern challenges, such as the increased workload of Mawlawis (teachers and mosque imams), who replaced Labbais in many cases, further marginalized Arwi education due to their unfamiliarity and disinterest in the language.

Cultural Resilience of Arwi

Despite its decline, iconic Arwi literary works like *Rastal Malai* and *Talai Fatiha* continue to be cherished and recited by Moors in Sarandib and Arwi-speaking Muslims in coastal Tamil Nadu. This resilience demonstrates that Arwi has not been entirely forgotten or erased from cultural memory, despite the societal shifts and educational transformations.

Factors Contributing to Arwi's Decline

Several factors have contributed to the decline of Arwi:

- **Shift to Secular Education**: The introduction of compulsory secular education reduced the emphasis on religious education in Arwi.
- **Changing Parental Attitudes**: Many Muslim parents no longer view enrollment in

Maktabs as a sacred duty, prioritizing secular education instead.

- **Lack of Institutional Support**: The dwindling number of Maktabs and the replacement of traditional teachers with Mawlawis unfamiliar with Arwi contributed to its neglect.

Despite these challenges, the enduring cultural significance of Arwi works underscores its legacy and the ongoing efforts to preserve its language and heritage among the Arwi-speaking communities.

Clarification on Arabic-Tamil (Arwi) vs. Tamil in the Dravidian Script

There is a common misconception that Arabic-Tamil, also known as Arwi, is synonymous with Tamil written in the Dravidian script with the addition of Arabic words. This view is not only erroneous but also potentially damaging to the understanding and development of Arwi. Here's a clear distinction between the two:

1. **Arabic-Tamil (Arwi)**:
   - **Script**: Written entirely in the Arabic script with appropriate diacritical marks.
   - **Language Basis**: Primarily Tamil in terms of grammar and structure.
   - **Incorporation of Arabic**: Includes Arabic loanwords and expressions that are integrated into Tamil sentences but are never used in standard Tamil.
   - **Emphasis**: The emphasis is on writing in the Arabic script while maintaining Tamil linguistic rules and structure.
2. **Tamil in the Dravidian Script**:
   - **Script**: Uses the Dravidian script (Tamil script) for writing.
   - **Language Basis**: Purely Tamil in terms of both vocabulary and grammar, avoiding significant influence from other languages like Arabic.
   - **Purist Movement**: In Tamil Nadu, there has been a resurgence of purist movements favoring the use of native

Tamil words over Sanskrit loanwords, showcasing a preference for maintaining linguistic purity.

Importance of Clarity

It's crucial to differentiate between these two forms as misunderstanding could lead to:

- **Misrepresentation**: Misleading portrayals could undermine the unique cultural and linguistic heritage of Arwi.
- **Educational Impact**: Misconceptions might discourage the learning and preservation of Arwi, particularly among younger generations.

Arabic-Tamil (Arwi) is distinctively characterized by its use of the Arabic script and integration of Arabic vocabulary into Tamil grammar. This unique linguistic fusion highlights its cultural significance and should be accurately understood and preserved to maintain its legacy among Arwi-speaking communities.

Campaign Against Arwi: Impact and Response

The history of Arwi, or Arabic-Tamil, has been marked by both significant contributions and challenges, particularly in the face of criticism and opposition. Here’s a detailed look at the campaign against Arwi and its consequences:

Criticism and Impact

1. **Modern Muslim Writers' Criticism**: In Tamil Nadu, some modern Muslim writers began criticizing Arwi, emphasizing the importance of Tamil over Arwi. This stance created a misconception that Arwi was less worthy of study or practice compared to Tamil.
2. **Role of B. Dawud Shah**: B. Dawud Shah, a prominent Tamil writer and editor of "Darul Islam" publications, played a pivotal role in attacking Arwi. He advocated against its use and propagation, which significantly

influenced public opinion and contributed to a decline in its prominence.

3. **Effects on Community**: The anti-Arwi sentiment fostered by Dawud Shah and his followers led to a gradual decline in the use and appreciation of Arwi among Tamil-speaking Muslims. This shift was not only linguistic but also had implications for religious and cultural practices within the community.

Response and Reflection

1. **Continued Advocacy**: Despite the opposition, there were individuals and publishers dedicated to preserving and promoting Arwi. Their efforts were crucial in maintaining the language's presence through the publication of Arwi books, which served to educate and inform the community about its cultural and religious significance.
2. **Cultural and Religious Importance**: Arwi represents a unique fusion of Tamil grammar

with Arabic vocabulary, primarily used for religious texts and teachings. Its preservation is essential not only for linguistic diversity but also for the continuation of religious traditions and teachings among Tamil-speaking Muslims.

3. **Historical Context**: Understanding the historical context of the criticism against Arwi helps in appreciating the challenges faced by linguistic and cultural minorities in preserving their heritage amidst changing societal norms and preferences.

The campaign against Arwi, spearheaded by figures like B. Dawud Shah, underscored the complexities surrounding linguistic identity and cultural preservation among Tamil-speaking Muslims. Despite these challenges, ongoing efforts to recognize and safeguard Arwi remain crucial for maintaining the linguistic and religious heritage of the community.

Impact of Anti-Arwi Campaigns: Analysis and Consequences

The campaign against Arwi, spearheaded by figures like Ghulam of Hagigi Sons and others, had profound implications for the Tamil-speaking Muslim community in Tamil Nadu. Here's a detailed exploration of its impact:

Criticism and Attacks

1. **Ghulam of Hagigi Sons**: As the owner of a printing and publishing house in Attur, Salem District, Ghulam embarked on a relentless campaign against Arwi. He not only criticized the language itself but also attacked the religious scholars ('Ulama) associated with it.
2. **Lack of Knowledge**: Critics like Ghulam, lacking proficiency in Arabic or Arwi, nevertheless issued judgments (Fatwas) disparaging Arwi and its literature. This further exacerbated the campaign's impact,

spreading misinformation among the community.

3. **Discrediting Literature**: Beyond linguistic criticism, the campaign extended to discrediting the content of Arwi books authored by esteemed scholars. This led to doubts among the common Muslims about the authenticity and reliability of Arwi literature and religious teachings it contained.

Harmful Effects

1. **Decline in Prestige**: The sustained campaign eroded the prestige and importance that Arwi once held within the community. This decline was exacerbated by the withdrawal of interest among Muslim women in learning Arwi, impacting its transmission across generations.
2. **Impact on Religious Education**: By discrediting Arwi literature and religious teachings, the campaign indirectly affected the religious education and cultural identity of Tamil-speaking Muslims. It shifted focus

away from traditional teachings preserved in Arwi texts.

3. **Response from Scholars**: Scholars like Mawlavi B.A. Khalilur Rahman Riyazi took legal action to counter the false narratives and restore confidence in Arwi and its educational value. Such efforts were crucial in mitigating the damage caused by the anti-Arwi campaigns.

The anti-Arwi campaigns led by individuals like Ghulam of Hagigi Sons had far-reaching consequences for the Tamil-speaking Muslim community in Tamil Nadu. They not only undermined the linguistic heritage of Arwi but also challenged its religious and cultural significance. Despite these challenges, ongoing efforts by scholars and community leaders remain essential to preserve and promote Arwi as an integral part of Tamil Muslim identity and religious education.

The abandonment of Arwi among Tamil-speaking Muslims in Sarandib and Tamil Nadu has had profound consequences for their religious life. In earlier times, Arwi was cherished by Muslim women who considered it a sacred duty to learn and teach it, using Arwi for studying Islamic theology, jurisprudence (Fiqh), and religious texts. In coastal areas, nearly all Muslim women were proficient in Arwi.

One of the most detrimental effects of discontinuing Arwi is the void it left, now filled by obscene and vulgar Tamil journals. These publications pose a significant threat to the moral values of their readers, particularly educated Muslim women who are major subscribers. A glance at these magazines reveals content that undermines the cherished moral principles of Muslim society.

Furthermore, the knowledge of Arwi facilitated easier recitation of the Holy Qur'an, especially for women. Its decline has left many Muslims in predominantly Tamil regions unable to read the Qur'an properly. Some have resorted to writing Qur'anic verses in Tamil or Sinhala scripts and reciting them with flawed pronunciation, a practice considered objectionable. Similarly, religious practices like Dhikr (remembrance of Allah), Awrad (recitals), and Manaqib (tributes to saints), traditionally performed in Arwi, are now conducted using Arabic in Tamil or Sinhala scripts.

Several factors have contributed to the decline of Arwi. Firstly, modern education systems overwhelm Muslim children with a heavy school curriculum, leaving them no time to learn Arwi. This loss is exacerbated by misguided campaigns and statements from certain modern Muslim writers lacking religious grounding, as mentioned earlier. Additionally, negligence from some 'Ulama who are themselves unfamiliar with Arwi has also played a role.

Another significant factor is the adoption of the Silsilatun-Nizamiyyah syllabus in religious educational institutions across Tamil Nadu. This syllabus, introduced from North India in the early 20th century and named after Mullā Nizamuddin of Darul Ulum Firangi Mahal, Lucknow, does not include Arwi. Similarly, in Sarandib, Arabic colleges have also shifted towards this syllabus in recent decades, contributing to the marginalization of Arwi. Despite its historical role in these regions, the influence of Arwi in religious education has steadily diminished over the past fifty years due to these developments.

Several factors have led to the decline of Arwi. Firstly, the introduction of the Silsilatun-Nizamiyyah syllabus in Tamil Nadu's Arabic Madrasahs, imported from North India in the early 20th century, excluded Arwi from its curriculum. Teachers trained in North Indian Madrasahs, unfamiliar with Arwi's language and culture, further diminished its presence in these institutions.

Secondly, some 'Ulama in Tamil Nadu, lacking familiarity with Arwi's unique letters and symbols, actively discouraged its teaching, possibly due to their own lack of expertise.

Thirdly, improved transport links between North and South India increased contact with Urdu, the predominant language of North Indian Muslims, sidelining Arwi which was subsequently neglected and eventually forgotten.

Fourthly, the widespread use of Sanskrit-origin letters like ja, sha, and ha in Tamil script partly replaced the need for Arwi's distinct characters, eroding its significance.

Additionally, the decline of traditional Arwi teaching Maktabs and their replacement of Arwi-supportive Labbais with less knowledgeable Mawlawis contributed significantly to Arwi's decline.

Lastly, the establishment of modern Tamil printing presses streamlined the production of Tamil books but complicated the lithographic process necessary for printing Arwi texts, causing delays and hindrances.

The decline of Arwi was hastened by the diminishing number of skilled scribes, known as Katibs, who painstakingly copied texts due to inadequate compensation for their laborious work. This gradual decline in skilled artisans led to a preference for printing religious texts in Tamil rather than Arwi, which was a much more complex and time-consuming process. The introduction of fast transport facilities connecting North and South India also contributed to the neglect of Arwi, as closer contact with Urdu-speaking North Indian Muslims led to a decline in interest and usage of Arwi, ultimately leading to its near oblivion.

Expressions of concern regarding the abandonment of Arwi in Arabic Madrasahs emerged later. Figures like Saint 'Abdul Karim Hadrat, founder-principal of an-Nurul-Muhammadiyyah, advocated for the reinstatement of Arwi as a medium of instruction, emphasizing its vital role in Islamic education. Despite these efforts, the practical implementation of Arwi as a medium of instruction faced challenges and was not fully realized before the premature death of advocates like Hadrat at an early age.

Shaykh Adam Hadrat, another esteemed scholar, also stressed the necessity of reviving Arwi, underscoring its importance in preserving Islamic knowledge. Even in later correspondence, scholars like Hadrat Diya'uddin Amani continued to highlight the advantages of Arwi in learning Islamic subjects, reflecting ongoing concerns within the community about the consequences of neglecting Arwi education.

The push for reintroducing Arwi in Arabic colleges gained momentum through efforts by influential figures like Amani Hadrat and Muhammad Ghani Hadrat of Madurai, among others. At a conference attended by leaders such as Shaykh Nayagam 'Abdul Qadir, Amani Hadrat stressed the importance of integrating Arwi into educational curricula to preserve Islamic knowledge. Despite initial efforts, the sustained use of Arwi faced challenges, as observed when visiting Amani Hadrat's Madrasah posthumously, where Arwi books were found unused due to student disinterest.

Shaykh Nayagam 'Abdul Qadir, shortly before his passing in 1975, appealed to scholars in Sarandib and Tamil Nadu to revive Arwi. He mandated its study in the primary Maktabs and colleges under his supervision, recognizing its critical role in maintaining Islamic heritage. Similarly, Shaykhul Bahjah Muhammad Ajwad al Balqami of Bahjatul Ibrahimiyyah Arabic College, Galle, lamented Muslim neglect of Arwi in a 1985 letter, urging scholars to prioritize its revival. Shamsuddin Hadrat of Vedalai, a respected scholar, also advocated for Arwi's resurgence during his tenure at Ghafuriyyah Arabic College, Mahargama, Colombo.

Abū Bakr Hadrat, former Principal of Baqiyat Arabic College, Vellore, along with Rahmatullah Hadrat of Arabic College, Nidur, and Diyaruddin Hadrat, former Principal of another Arabic College, responded positively to efforts aimed at reintroducing Arwi in Tamil Nadu's Arabic Colleges. Some of these scholars visited Madrasatul 'Arttsiyyah, Kilakarai, specifically to support this initiative.

H.S. Ismall, former Speaker of the Parliament of Ceylon and Vice-President of 'Artusiyyatul Qadiriyyah Association, Sarandib, expressed deep concern in a 1967 letter to the writer about the current generation's neglect of Arwi. He highlighted the detrimental impact on Quranic recitation skills and fervently advocated for its revival.

The decline of Arwi represents an irreparable loss to the Muslim community. Originating from historical necessity, Arwi evolved into the mother-tongue of Tamil Muslims, enriched with extensive religious literature. Its descent into obscurity, as outlined earlier, is profoundly regrettable.

To revive the Arwi tradition, several strategies can be considered:

1. Publishing short pamphlets that emphasize the importance of preserving Arwi, its cultural significance, and the benefits it offers to Muslims.
2. Collecting and reprinting all available Arwi books, including unpublished manuscripts, to ensure their preservation and accessibility.
3. Making Arwi a mandatory subject in all madrasahs across Sarandib and Tamil Nadu to secure its future relevance and usage.

These steps aim to restore Arwi's prominence and ensure its survival as a vital part of Tamil Muslim heritage.

Additional measures to revive Arwi include:

4. Reprinting religious and secular Arwi books in an appealing format for schoolchildren.
5. Establishing primary schools and kindergartens with Arwi as the medium of instruction in Arwi-speaking regions.
6. Encouraging scholars and students to maintain correspondence in Arwi.
7. Reintroducing Arwi periodicals and magazines.
8. Organizing essay competitions in Arwi for students.
9. Encouraging present-day Muslims in Sarandib and Tamil Nadu who are neglecting Arwi to use it in their daily lives.
10. Conducting lectures, meetings, and conferences in Arwi-speaking areas to raise awareness about its importance and promote its development.

Implementing these suggestions is both feasible and essential for the preservation and revitalization of Arwi.

A fervent appeal was made by M.B. Noordeen, Director of Education in Sri Lanka, in his report, acknowledging the relentless efforts of Sarandib Moors to preserve Arwi. He urges Muslims to recognize the urgency of continuing these efforts to achieve tangible outcomes (refer to appendix 34 for details).

A.M.A. Aziz, a respected Moor, expressed deep concern over the decline of Arwi in a letter to Sayyid Muhammad Hasan, a Research Scholar in Madras, just months before his passing. His passionate plea for cooperation among scholars underscores his unwavering commitment to Arwi until the end of his life (see appendices 44 and 45 for more on A.M.A. Aziz and Sir Rāzik Farid).

A.M.A. Aziz conveyed a message to the Islamic Tamil Literature Conference held at Kalmunai, Sarandib, on July 2, 1976. He emphasized that Arwi represents a unique fusion of two significant languages—Semitic-Arabic and Dravidian-Tamil—and described it as a historic phenomenon that cannot be overlooked. Aziz viewed Arwi as a cultural bridge connecting Muslims in Sarandib with those in Tamil Nadu. He passionately advocated for the preservation, research, and development of Arwi, reflecting the deep-seated desire of Sarandib's devout Muslims to revive and promote the language, a sentiment less prominent among Tamil Nadu's Muslims.

Arwi, historically cherished by noble scholars and revered saints, served as a remedy for various social ailments over centuries. It enjoyed widespread support from both the masses and intellectuals, underscoring its critical role in the religious life and unity of Arwi-speaking Muslims. Understanding the significance attributed to Lisanul Arwi by visionary leaders of the past holds immense potential for the community's future.

Conclusion

The exploration of Arwi presented in this book reveals a narrative of resilience, decline, and hope. Arwi, a language born from the interplay of Arabic and Tamil influences among South Indian and Sri Lankan Muslims, once served as a vital conduit for religious education, cultural expression, and community cohesion. Its unique script and vocabulary facilitated the transmission of Islamic teachings and cultural practices across generations, enriching the fabric of regional identity.

However, as societal dynamics evolved with modern education systems and cultural shifts, Arwi faced neglect and marginalization. Educational reforms, linguistic assimilation, and socio-economic changes contributed to its decline, jeopardizing its status as a living language among younger generations.

Nevertheless, amidst these challenges, voices of scholars, educators, and community leaders have emerged advocating for the revival of Arwi. They emphasize its intrinsic value in preserving religious traditions, fostering cultural continuity, and reconnecting communities with their linguistic heritage. Efforts to reintroduce Arwi into educational curricula, reprint its literary works, and promote its use in everyday life reflect a growing recognition of its significance.

Looking ahead, the journey to revive Arwi requires concerted efforts across multiple fronts – educational institutions, community initiatives, and scholarly research. By rekindling interest in Arwi, promoting its study, and integrating it into contemporary discourse, there is potential to rejuvenate this invaluable cultural and linguistic legacy.

This book serves as a call to action, urging readers to recognize the importance of Arwi in the broader context of South Asian Muslim identity and cultural diversity. It underscores the imperative of preserving linguistic heritage as a means of safeguarding cultural pluralism and enriching global understanding.

In conclusion, the story of Arwi is not just about a language's past glory or present challenges; it is a testament to resilience and the enduring quest to preserve cultural and linguistic diversity in an ever-changing world.

References

Ajwad, M. A. (1985). Letter to [Author's Name]. Bahjatul Ibrahimiyyah Arabic College.

Al-Attas, S. M. N. (1993). Islam and secularism. Kuala Lumpur: ISTAC.

Al-Dimasyqi, A.-I. A.-N. (2016). Syarh Shahih Muslim. Dar al-Kutub al-`Ilmiyah.

al-Maraghi, M. (2002). Tafsir al-Maraghi. Beirut: Darul Fikir.

Al-Nurul-Muhammadiyyah Arabic Madrasah. (n.d.). An-Nurul-Muhammadiyyah.

Al-Qaradawi, Y. (2010). Islam an introduction. Kuala Lumpur: Islamic Book Trust.

al-Qurtubi, A. A. M. ibn A. (2014). Tafsir al-Qurtubi (Vol. 20). Beirut: Dar al-Kutub al-'Ilmiyah.

Al-Qushayri, I. (2018). Tafsir al-Qushayri. Dar Ihya' al-Turath al-Arabi.

Al-Rāzī, F. (2000). Al-Tafsīr al-Kabīr aw Mafātih al-Gayb, Vol. VII. Dar Al-Hadith.

Al-Sya'rawi, A.-I. A.-M. (2007). Tafsir Al-Sya'rawi. Qitha' al-Saqafah wa al-Kutub.

Al-Syawkani, M. bin A. (2014). Fath al-Qadir al-Jami' baina Fannai al-Riwayah wa al-Dirayah min 'Ilm al-Tafsir, Vol. 5. Dar Ibnu Hazim.

Al-Thabathaba'i. (1987). Tafsir Al-Mizan. Islamic Publications Office.

Al-Zuhaily, W. (2009). Al-Tafsir al-Munir fi al-Aqidah wa al-Syariah wa al-Manhaj. Dar al-Fikr.

APS (Applied Social Psychology). (2017). The Role of Religion in Prejudice Enablement and Reduction. Retrieved December 26, 2022, from https://sites.psu.edu/aspsy/2017/09/28/the-role-of-religion-in-prejudice-enablement-and-reduction/

Arwi Muslims. (1978). *World Islamic Tamil Literature Souvenir*. Jamal Muhammad College.

Aziz, A. M. A. (1966). *Arabu - Tamil, Engal Anbu Tamil*. Diamond Printers.

Bakhshi Hazrat 'Alī Aḥmed and Rizwānur Raḥmān. (2012). Glimpses of the Holy Qur'ān. (New

Chelini-Pont, B. (2013). Relationship between Stereotyping and the Place of Religion in the Public Sphere. In J. Svartvik, Jesper & Wiren (Ed.), Religious Stereotyping and Interreligious Relations (pp. 75–84). Palgrave Macmillan.

Geertz, C. (1977). The Interpretation of Cultures. Basic Books.

Geertz, C. (2013). Religion as a cultural system. In Anthropological Approaches to the Study of Religion (pp. 1–46). https://doi.org/10.4324/9781315017570

Hanafi, H. (2000). Islam in the modern world: Religion, ideology and development vol. I. Cairo: Dar Kabaa.

Hanafi, H. (2006). Culture and civilizations, conflict or dialogue? Vol. I the meridian thought. Cairo: Book Center for Publishing.

Hijazi, M. A. (1986). *Durrul Mukthar*. Cairo Print.

Jafari, F. (2020). Theological knowledge in Islamic mysticism and gnosticism." Kanz Philosophia A Journal for Islamic Philosophy and Mysticism 6(2). DOI: https://doi.org/10.20871/kpjipm.v6i2.92.

Karama, M. J., & Khater, N. A. (2020). Educational peace theory in the holy qur᾽an. Al-Bayān – Journal of Qur᾽ān and Ḥadīth Studies, 18, 138–154. http://scholar.ppu.edu/bitstream/handle/123456789/2214/1.pdf?sequence=1&isAllowed=y

Khairulnizam, M., & Saili, S. (2009). Inter-faith dialogue: The qur'anic and prophetic perspective. Journal of Usuluddin, 9(2), 65–94.

Khaldun, I. (2015). Muqaddimah. Cairo: Dar-Ibnu al-Aitam.

Khan, A. (n.d.). *Muslims in India*. Lucknow.

Kidwai, Salim. (1996). Hindustani Mufassirein Awr Unki' Arabi Tafsirein (in Urdu) .(New Delhi:Maktaba Jamiah).

Kokan, Moḥammad Yousuf. (1960). Arabic and Persian in Carnatic, (Madras: Hafiza House).

Ma'roof M M M. (1995). *Spoken Tamil dialect of the Muslims of Sri Lanka: Language as Identity classifier*. Islamic Studies 34 (4).

Muhammad Hasan, S. (n.d.). [Title of Report]. Muslim Educational Conference.

Nashir, H. (2015). Understanding the ideology of Muhammadiyah. Muhammadiyah University Press.

Nieuwkerk, K. van, LeVine, M., & Stokes, M. (2016). Islam and popular culture. University of Texas Press.

Noordeen, M. B. (n.d.). [Title of Report]. Muslim Educational Conference.

Patji, A. R. (1991). The Arabs of Surabaya: a study of sociocultural integration. Canberra: Australian National University.

Putra, A. D., Purnomo, D., & Utomo, A. W. (2019). Sociological study of harmony in diversity: Lessons from Salatiga. Walisongo: Jurnal Penelitian Sosial Keagamaan, 27(1), 69–98. 10.21580/ws.27.1.3504

Rahman, M. A. (1978). *World Islamic Tamil Literature Souvenir*. Jamal Muhammad College.

Ridwan, M., & Robikah, S. (2019). Ethical vision of the qur'an: Interpreting concept of the qur'anic sociology in developing religious harmony. Jurnal Ilmiah Islam Futura, 18(2), 308–326. http://dx.doi.org/10.22373/jiif.v19i2.5444

Saerozi, M. (2017). Dynamics of the development of istiqomah mosque in front of a church in Ungaran Central Java Indonesia. Journal of Indonesian Islam, 11(02), 423–458. 10.15642/JIIS.2017.11.2.423-458

Saged, A. A. (2021). Honoring the human self with a world peace study in the light of purposes the holy quran. Quranika: Journal of Libahuts Qur'an, 19(2), 223–234.

Shareef, Moḥammed Muṣṭafa and Bad'iuddin Ṣabri. (2008). Development of Tafseer Literature in India, (Hyderabad: Osmania University).

Shihab, M. Q. (2004). Tafsir al-mishbah. Jakarta: Lentera Hati.

Shu'aib, Tayka. (1993). Arabic, Arwi and Persian in Sarandib and Tamil Nadu, (Chennai: Imaamul Aroos Trust).

Thabari, I. J. (1999). Tafsir al Thabari. Kairo: Dar al Fikr.

Zamakhsyari, M. I. U. al. (2012). Al-kassyaf 'an haqaiq al-tanzil wa 'uyun al-ta'wil fi wujuh al-ta'wil. Cairo: Dar al-Hadis.

Zubair, K M A Aḥamed. (2010). *Tamil-Arabic Relationship*, ed. John Samuel G, (Chennai:The Institute of Asian Studies Press).

Zubair, K M A Ahamed. (2012). *Eminent Scholars of Sheik Sadaqathullah Appa's Family and their contribution to Arabic and Islamic Studies,* (in Arabic), Thaqafatul ḥind 54, (3&4).

Zubair, K M A Ahamed. (2013). *Qasaid al-Madaih al-Nabaviyya fi Tamil Nadu,* (in Arabic), Thaqafatul ḥind 64, (4).

Zubair, K M A Aḥamed. (2017). Prophet's Panegyrics in Arabic Literature, (Moldova: Lambert Academic Publishing).

Zubair, K M A Aḥamed. et al. (2024). Islamic-Arab Morals, Virtues and Characters In Arabic-Tamil Novel "Madinatun Nuhas" or "Tamirapattanam". Ijaz Arabi Journal of Arabic Learning, 7(1). 208-217. https://doi.org/10.18860/ijazarabi.v7i1.23157

Printed by Books on Demand GmbH, Norderstedt / Germany